BrandedAgent

The 7 Strategies Workbook

Becoming
First In Mind

Welcome to the **Branded Agent Workbook**. You may be new to real estate or you may have decided that your real estate career needs a makeover. Congratulations, you've picked the best place to start. The Branded Agent approach to top production laid out in this workbook will change the way you look at selling real estate. Think your way through the 3 steps of discovering, building, and being your own powerful personal brand. Learn to use the 7 personal branding strategies common among top producers nationwide. Create a consistent marketing plan that reaches the right target market audience. The old sales model is broken. In fact, it never really worked. Buyers and sellers have been over-sold and spun into submission. They don't want to be sold *by* you, they want to be sold *on* you.

In sales, people choose the agent who they are familiar with. They pick the agent they like, believe, and trust. They overwhelmingly call **the agent first in mind**. 75% of buyers and sellers use the services of the only agent that they call. How do you make sure that you are the agent who always gets that one call? You use the proven dynamics of branding in this workbook to position yourself as the familiar market expert of choice. Discover what makes you uniquely relevant and compelling. Align yourself with the perfect target market niche.

There are no gimmicks in here, no schtick, and no shortcuts. To create your own powerful personal real estate brand you must uncover your own authentic passion and build a real estate career around it. This workbook is about you, and so is your real estate success. As you progress through the workbook you elevate "you" to "You Inc."—an unforgettable brand. This is the work that herd doesn't do. The 7 strategies will move you out of the herd and ignite your successful and rewarding career.

Branded Agent Workbook Table of Contents

Personal Brand Discovery

Uncovering the Authentic Passion of You Inc.

Passion: A strong and barely controllable emotion, an intense desire or enthusiasm for something.

1. What are the types of things or ideas that you are passionate about?
   1._____
   2._____
   3._____
   4._____
   5._____

2. What would you do every day if you didn't need to work or worry about money?
   1._____
   2._____
   3._____
   4._____

3. If you could pick only one activity to do for the rest of your life, what would it be?
   1._____
   2._____
   3._____

Doodle Box

Your Qualities

Qualities: Distinctive attribute or characteristic possessed by someone or something.

4. What are your unique qualities?

   1._____
   2._____
   3._____
   4._____
   5._____

Characteristics: Feature belonging typically to a person, place, or thing and serving to identify it.

5. What are a few of your most distinct personal characteristics?

   1._____
   2._____
   3._____
   4._____
   5._____

6. What types of things do you get most complimented or commended on?

   1._____
   2._____
   3._____
   4._____

Doodle Box

People enjoy working with agents who they like, trust and believe. Leveraging the things on the previous page that make you relevant and compelling to a target market audience is crucial to top production. The good things that set you apart are the things that will help make you first in mind.

Your Skills and Abilities

7. What are your greatest skills and abilities?

1._____

2._____

3._____

4._____

5._____

8. What is distinct about these skills and abilities?

1._____

2._____

3._____

4._____

5._____

9. How do these skills and abilities add value to others?

_____

_____

_____

_____

Doodle Box

List praise and comments that you consistently receive from satisfied clients, managers, peers, family, and coworkers.

_____

_____

_____

_____

_____

You Inc.: Term used for a person that is perceived as an unforgettably relevant commodity.

What is the current market perception of your brand?

_____

_____

_____

_____

_____

What is your fear of being true to your authentic identity?

_____

_____

_____

_____

List and describe the authentic identity and message of You Inc.?

    1._____

    2._____

    3._____

    4._____

    5._____

_____

_____

_____

Your Core Values

Core Value: A principle that guides your internal conduct as well as your relationship with the external world. Core values are usually summarized in a mission statement.

10. *What are your own core values?*

1._____
2._____
3._____
4._____
5._____

11. What are you most proud of?

1._____
2._____
3._____
4._____
5._____

12. What do you want to be remembered for?

1._____
2._____
3._____
4._____
5._____

Doodle Box

Write your Eulogy:

Passion, qualities, skills, and values are the nucleus of your personal brand. In looking at what makes up your true authentic self you get a better understanding of where to go. The number one regret that people have at the end of their lives is that they didn't live life that they wanted to, and instead lived the life that others wanted them to. Write the eulogy that you want given at the end of your life.

_____

_____

_____

_____

_____

_____

_____

_____

_____

_____

_____

_____

Write a Mission statement for You Inc.

What do I really love to do? When am I at my best? What are my natural talents? If I had unlimited time and resources, I would? What is my most important future contribution? What is the quality or attribute that I admire most in people? What problem can I help fix? Where can I work on resolving problems that intrigues me?

Try this format: Verb, Target, Outcome.

_____

_____

_____

_____

_____

_____

_____

_____

_____

_____

_____

Target Market Discovery

Aligning Passion and Target Market

Real Estate is a relationship business. A strong authentic relationship with your target market makes you the agent first in mind and creates a rewarding career. List the groups below that revolve around the things you are passionate about.

Organizations, Clubs, Groups and Associations:

1._____
2._____
3._____
4._____
5._____

Offline Networks:

1._____
2._____
3._____
4._____
5._____

Online Networks, Websites, Blogs:

1._____
2._____
3._____
4._____
5._____

Doodle Box

Non-profits and Cooperatives:

1._____
2._____
3._____
4._____
5._____

Leagues and Recreational:

1._____
2._____
3._____
4._____
5._____

Businesses, Companies, Institutions:

1._____
2._____
3._____
4._____
5._____

Gatherings, Events, Activities:

1._____
2._____
3._____
4._____
5._____

Faith, Political Organizations:

1._____
2._____
3._____
4._____
5._____

Schools, Colleges, Universities:

1._____
2._____
3._____
4._____
5._____

Restaurants, Bars, Coffee Shops, Hangouts:

1._____
2._____
3._____
4._____
5._____

Given the groups above, answer these questions:

What publications and media are relevant to these groups?

1._____
2._____
3._____
4._____
5._____
6._____
7._____
8._____

What are the websites and blogs they use?

1._____
2._____
3._____
4._____
5._____
6._____
7._____

Where do the members of these groups gather, live, work, play, practice, learn, and socialize?

1._____

2._____

3._____

4._____

5._____

Define Your Target Market Niche?

_____

_____

_____

_____

_____

_____

_____

Gut Check

Do you fit into the special target market you have chosen?

☐ Yes. This niche fits my personality, interests, and values perfectly.

☐ Somewhat, I need to refine my focus. With some adjustments to my brand or to the niche, this could work. (Use the lines below to describe the changes you might make.)

_____

_____

_____

_____

_____

☐ Not at all. I would be compromising my personal lifestyle, values, and or authentic self to fit into this market. Go back to page 3 and start again.

Target Market Analysis Worksheet

Use the following three step formula to determine if your chosen target market can support your business. The commission number is an estimated average, commissions are always negotiable. The final number reflects the number of homes you would need to sell to sustain your business and reach your goals.

1. Average Home Price **×** Average Commission **×** split = Average Commission

(example) $450,000 **×** 3% **×** 65% = $8,775
(example) $250,000 **×** 3% **×** 65% = $4,875

$_____ × _____% _____% = $_____

2. Income Goal ÷ Average Commission = Annual Transaction Goal

(example) $160,000 ÷ $8,775 = 18 Homes
(example) $100,000 ÷ $4,875 = 21 Homes

$_____ × $_____ = _____Homes

Doodle Box

3. Transaction Goal ÷ Market Share Goal ÷ 2 (commission sides per sale)
= Target Market Property Sales Needed for Agent To Reach Goal.

(example) 18 ÷ 20% ÷ 2 = 45 sales
(example) 21 ÷ 20% ÷ 2 = 53 sales

_____ ÷ _____% ÷ 2 = _____sales

4. Property Sales Needed for Agent to Reach Goal ÷ Market Turnover
Rate = Total Target Market Properties Needed to Reach Goals.

(example) 45 ÷ .08 (turnover %) = 563 Target Homes Needed
(example) 53 ÷ .08 (turnover %) = 663 Target Homes Needed

_____ ÷ _____% = _____ homes needed

Doodle Box

Knowing Your Target Market

Researching Your Market Niche

Create a blueprint of your market to use in building a consistent brand. What are the best opportunities to position You Inc. for maximum market engagement?

Common Interests That Define the Target Market:

1._____
2._____
3._____
4._____
5._____

Target Market Unique and Common Qualities:

1._____
2._____
3._____
4._____
5._____

Target Market Common Values:

1._____
2._____
3._____
4._____
5._____

Doodle Box

Target Market Common Skills and Abilities:

1._____

2._____

3._____

4._____

5._____

Target Market Style:

1._____

2._____

3._____

4._____

5._____

Important Target Market Issues and Topics:

1._____

2._____

3._____

4._____

5._____

Target Market Activities:

1._____

2._____

3._____

4._____

5._____

Target Market Preferred Recreation:

1._____

2._____

3._____

4._____

5._____

Target Market Popular Events:

1._____
2._____
3._____
4._____
5._____

Target Market Hotspots:

1._____
2._____
3._____
4._____
5._____

Target Market Preferred Charitable Organizations:

1._____
2._____
3._____
4._____
5._____

Target Market Preferred Schools and Colleges:

1._____
2._____
3._____
4._____
5._____

Target Market Preferred Publications and Media:

1._____
2._____
3._____
4._____
5._____

Target Market Preferred Websites:

1._____
2._____
3._____
4._____
5._____

Target Market Preferred Blogs:

1._____
2._____
3._____
4._____
5._____

Target Market Preferred Offline Networks:

1._____
2._____
3._____
4._____
5._____

Target Market Preferred Online Networks:

1._____
2._____
3._____
4._____
5._____

Other about Your Target Market:

_____
_____
_____
_____
_____

What are the best groups that you can get involved with now?

Top Target Market Networks and Groups:

1. _____
2. _____
3. _____
4. _____
5. _____
6. _____
7. _____
8. _____
9. _____
10. _____

Steps To Get Engaged In Each Above Group:

1. _____
2. _____
3. _____
4. _____
5. _____
6. _____
7. _____
8. _____
9. _____
10. _____

Doodle Box

Building Your Brand With 7 Strategies

Strategy 1: Style

Appearance

People label, judge and categorize others. It's not right to judge a book by its cover but it's what people do. It's how we manage the onslaught of activity in our hurried lives. Use it to your brand advantage. Be authentic in brand appearance and comportment. This may mean an aligned makeover, but you're worth it. Since people are going to label you make it easy for them. Categorize yourself for others visually by how you act and what you wear. Make people understand your brand identity and message through your style.

Note: Up to 20% of personal attraction is based on self-confidence. Another 40% of it is based on good oral communication style, and the last 40% is attributed to overall visual appearance.

Wardrobe:_____

_____

_____

_____

Things to add and change to your appearance and styling

1._____

2._____

3._____

4._____

5._____

Doodle Box

Comportment:_____

_____

_____

_____

Things to add and change to your presentation and approach:

      1._____

      2._____

      3._____

      4._____

      5._____

Stylists to call:

      1._____

      2._____

Photography

Let people get your identity and message immediately. Pictures do speak 1,000 words and tell the story of your brand, even at a glance. Establish brand identity and message with your photo. Align to target market. Use high definition. Be relevant and compelling. No mug shots.

Poses:

      1._____

      2._____

      3._____

      4._____

Locations:

      1._____

      2._____

      3._____

      4._____

Wardrobe:

1._____
2._____
3._____
4._____

Photographers to call:

1._____
2._____

Date for Shoot:

1._____

Colors

- **Black** is the color of authority and power.
- **White** is light, neutral, and pure.
- **Red** is emotionally intense and increases heart rate and breathing. Red is associated with passion, fury, and love.
- **Blue** evokes a sense of calmness and serenity. Recognized as the color of the sky and sea, blue evokes a sense of tranquility and causes the body to produce calming chemicals.
- **Green** is also calming, refreshing, and relaxing. Green is associated with the environment, health, and money (many banks use green).
- **Yellow** enhances concentration, and represents optimism, but can be hard on the eyes depending on the shade and amount used.
- **Purple** has historically been associated with royalty and luxury, and unfortunately, Barney.
- **Brown** is reliable, genuine, and earthy.

What corporate brand Color combinations are memorable to you and why:

1._____
2._____
3._____
4._____

What Color combinations work for both your style and identity and that of your target market:

_____

_____

_____

Your Color Scheme:

    1._____

Logos

A successful logo must:

1. Apply professional graphic and design fundamentals.
2. Function and display consistently across different marketing platforms.
3. Represent and convey your brand identity and message.
4. Create a memorable and compelling impression.
5. Create an association with your target market.

List logos of other companies that are memorable to you:

    1._____

    2._____

    3._____

    4._____

Why do these logos stand out to you?

_____

_____

_____

Do they each represent their respective company's message? How?

    1._____

    2._____

    3._____

    4._____

List ways to express your brand identity and message through a logo?

_____

_____

_____

_____

_____

The perfect logo to unite you with your target market would be:

_____

_____

_____

Logo Ideas:

Tagline:

A tagline literally lets you use words to communicate brand message. Taglines communicate targeted relevancy in a few well chosen unforgettable words.

Five ways to describe your target market audience?

1._____
2._____
3._____
4._____
5._____

What value and benefits do you provide them?

1._____
2._____
3._____
4._____
5._____

What words best articulate your unique brand?

1._____
2._____
3._____
4._____
5._____

How do your skills and abilities differ from the competition?

1._____
2._____
3._____
4._____
5._____

What emotions do you hope to evoke with your target audience?

1._____
2._____
3._____
4._____
5._____

What is the purpose of your branded business?

1._____
2._____
3._____
4._____
5._____

Build Taglines using the answers above:

1._____
2._____
3._____
4._____
5._____

Doodle Box

Narrative:

You must be able to articulate a compelling story of You Inc. A narrative explains your brand's benefits in depth. It builds an emotional bond between you and your target audience. A great story moves interested buyers and sellers beyond awareness to brand acceptance. It's about emotional connection not accolades or awards. People don't develop affinity with a brand that just brags about accomplishments. They connect with a relevant and intriguing story. Craft relatable copy around your story and explain values and benefits that make you the target market expert of choice. Pull your narrative from Pages 4 - 8 to tell the story of You Inc. Use what you uncovered in each set of questions about your passion, qualities, skills and abilities, and core values.

Passion

1._____

2._____

3._____

Qualities

1._____

2._____

3._____

4._____

Skills and abilities

1._____

2._____

3._____

4._____

Core Values

1._____

2._____

3._____

4._____

Write the third person story of you Inc. Keep in mind your relevance to your target audience.

_____

_____

_____

_____

_____

_____

_____

_____

_____

_____

_____

_____

_____

_____

_____

_____

_____

_____

_____

_____

_____

_____

_____

_____

Style Contacts: List the people who will help you master your steps to the branded style of You Inc.

1._____
2._____
3._____
4._____
5._____

Strategy 2: Internet Marketing

Website

Buyers and sellers want to find the target market expert and they want good comfortable search options. They want high resolution search results with smooth navigation and easy logistics.

☐ Website URL

_____

☐ Website Admin Co.

_____

Website Tabs:

☐ Search ☐ Blog ☐ About Market
☐ About You Inc. ☐ Featured listings

☐ Email Address:

_____

☐ Email Signature Company:

_____

☐ IDX Company:

_____

☐ SEO Company:

_____

☐ E-blast Company:

_____

E-blast Design: This should be the same consistent layout and design used for your advertising and direct mail postcard campaign.

☐ Website Tags and Google Adwords Search Term Keywords:

1._____

2._____

3._____

4._____

5._____

6._____

7._____

8._____

9._____

10._____

11._____

Internet Engagement and Activity
Three Listing Aggregators

☐ Zillow.com Profile Name

_____

   ☐ Ads?

_____

☐ Trulia.com Profile Name

_____

   ☐ Ads?

_____

☐ Realtor.com Profile Name

_____

   ☐ Ads?

_____

Four Online Networks

☐ Linkedin Profile Name

_____

☐ Facebook Profile Name

_____

☐ Twitter Profile Name

_____

☐ Google Plus Profile Name

_____

☐ Social Media Monitoring Tool

_____

Two Peer Networks

☐ Active Rain Profile Name

_____

☐ Branded Agent Network Profile Name

_____

Two Specific Target Market Online Networks
Join online networks in your target market. Pull them from answers on page 18. If there is not a good one, then start one!

☐ Target Market Online Network #1

_____

☐ Target Market Online Network #1

_____

☐ **Blog name**

_____

Internet Contacts: List the people who will help you master your branded website and your proactive activity on the other 9 targeted sites.

1._____
2._____
3._____
4._____
5._____

Strategy 3: Networking In Real Life

Target Market Networks:

Who you know is much more important to your real estate success than what you know. Real life networking builds a foundation of referral relationships and positions you as the obvious expert resource in your market.

Pull the 5 real life networks and groups you will proactively get engaged within your target market from page 13.

11._____

12._____

13._____

14._____

15._____

Launch a Network

☐ _____

_____

For each organization that you've listed, ask yourself the following:
1. Does this organization represent your target market and your brand? y/n
2. Are there ample opportunities to create the right relationships? y/n
3. Are the organization's values in line with yours and the target market? y/n
4. Is this an organization that you can authentically enjoy being a part of? y/n
5. Are there possibilities for leadership positions within the organization? y/n

If you've answered yes to three or more of these questions, then the organization presents the right opportunity to develop relationships, generating referral, and feed your passion.

Network Contacts: List the people who will help you master your steps to proactive and rewarding brand networking.

1._____

2._____

3._____

4._____

5._____

Strategy 4: Personal Brochure

The Branded Agent Personal Brochure is your tangible opportunity to comprehensively present your targeted brand style, identity, and message. Brand photography, colors, logos, taglines, style, design, and copywriting from strategy one are all combined in your brochure to impart your complete brand in one exposure.

What will be compelling to have people read further to learn about your brand story. Use the narrative from page 22 below to outline your personal brochure:

What are the 10 most important items and themes to put into your brochure.

1. _____
2. _____
3. _____
4. _____
5. _____
6. _____
7. _____
8. _____
9. _____
10. _____

What five things above from your narrative could be expanded on to better illustrate your passion, qualities, skills, and values in this longer piece.

1. _____
2. _____
3. _____
4. _____
5. _____

Doodle design your brochure ideas on the following page:

Brochure Page 1, front

Brochure Page 1, back

Brochure Page 3, interior right

Brochure Page 2, interior left

Brochure Contacts: List the people who will help you master the steps to a polished branded personal brochure.

1._____
2._____
3._____
4._____
5._____

Strategy 5: Advertising

Ads validate brand awareness created by your other consistent brand strategy exposures. You should put 15% of gross revenue back into personal branding each year. The majority of that will go toward advertising.

Estimated Annual Branding Budget: $_____

Branded Ad Template

A branded template saves you time and production cost over your career. Targeting and tailoring your campaign saves costs of reaching unnecessary recipients with ads that aren't relevant. It should be the same in style and design as your E-blasts and direct mailers. What information do you want to include on each template?

Ad Template:

Advertise Here:

List 4 targeted print publications to advertise in:

1._____Mo. Cost:_____

2._____Mo. Cost:_____

3._____Mo. Cost:_____

4._____Mo. Cost:_____

List 4 targeted online sites to advertise in:

1._____Mo. Cost:_____
2._____Mo. Cost:_____
3._____Mo. Cost:_____
4._____Mo. Cost:_____
5._____Mo. Cost:_____

For each publication ask yourself the following to evaluate the opportunity:

☐ Is this ad reaching my targeted market on a regular basis?

☐ Is my target market looking were this ad is?

☐ What is the shelf life and on screen time for this ad?

☐ Is this ad reaching a broader range of demographics than necessary for success and therefore more expensive?

☐ What is the cost of advertising Weekly/Monthly/Annually?

☐ Can the ad work within my budget?

☐ Does this ad and placement fall in line with the values of my niche market?

☐ How regularly do I need to advertise in this spot to be effective?

Business Card: Manintain brand style and design.

For Sale and Open House Signs: How much branding can you incoeporate into your signs

Advertising Contacts: List the people who will help you target and tailor your best branded advertising campaign.

1._____

2._____

3._____

4._____

5._____

Strategy 6: Direct Mail

The Branded Agent direct mail strategy includes postcards and newsletters mailed to your geographic or demographic target market. It is potent outreach because it achieves rare focused attention because of its delivery.

Postcards

☐ Direct mail House:

☐ Just Listed/Just Sold Design: Direct mail pieces are another consistent exposure securing your position as the active market leader of choice. Create with branded alignment, style, design, and layout to leverage the dynamic of consistent exposure from many directions.

☐ Ideas for Targeted Specific Postcard Mailings:

6. _____

7. _____

8. _____

9. _____

10. _____

Newsletter

☐ Direct Mail Newsletter Title:

_____

Direct Mail Newsletter Sections:

☐ Table of Contents ☐ Relevant Articles and News ☐ Market Sales Data

☐ Market Events ☐ Trends ☐ Networking Opportunities and Highlights

☐ Real Estate Tips ☐ Hot Topics ☐ Contact Information and Links

Newsletter Template

Letterhead Template

Header:

Footer:

Direct Mail Contacts

1._____

2._____

3._____

4._____

5._____

Strategy 7: Public Relations

Good public relations exposure is equivalent to a credible third party testimony. It is trusted exposure that positions You Inc. as a respected expert. An article that recognizes your brand through quotes or references is like a personal referral. Publicity is coveted recognition that means your brand is editorially worthy.

News and Media Outlets in Your Area:

Print

1. _____
2. _____
3. _____
4. _____
5. _____
6. _____
7. _____

Radio

1. _____
2. _____
3. _____
4. _____

TV

1. _____
2. _____
3. _____
4. _____
5. _____

Internet and Blogs

1. _____
2. _____
3. _____
4. _____
5. _____
6. _____

Press Releases

Every two to three weeks find a real estate industry or target market-centric story that is newsworthy and compelling. Write down ideas for intriguing press releases to work toward releasing.

1. _____
2. _____
3. _____
4. _____
5. _____
6. _____

Press Kit:

A well-designed press kit positions you best to generate attention grabbing media coverage. Don't be shy. You are newsworthy. Help journalists look good and become their real estate resource. Being perceived as editorially worthy by readers is a testimony to your brand and professionalism.

☐ Personal Photo ☐ References ☐ Press Release

☐ Articles and Newsletters ☐ Personal Brochure ☐ Marketing Examples

☐ Previous Media Coverage ☐ Speaking Topics ☐ FAQs

Public Relations Contacts

1._____
2._____
3._____
4._____
5._____

Being Your Brand

Strategy Maintenance Systems

What systems will/do you use to maintain each of the 7 strategies? The systems you choose to maintain the 7 strategies are there because we are all wired differently as to how we get things done. But you must use systems to actively maintain the strategies every week. They must keep things organized, polished, and consistent.

Strategy 1: Style

1. _____
2. _____
3. _____
4. _____

Strategy 2: Internet

1. _____
2. _____
3. _____
4. _____
5. _____
6. _____

Strategy 3: Network

1. _____
2. _____
3. _____
4. _____

Strategy 4: Brochure

1. _____
2. _____
3. _____
4. _____

Strategy 5: Advertising

1. _____
2. _____
3. _____
4. _____

Strategy 6: Direct Mail

1. _____
2. _____
3. _____
4. _____

Strategy 7: Public Relations

1. _____
2. _____
3. _____
4. _____

You Inc. Maintenance Systems

What systems will/do you use to maintain the three administrative areas of You Inc? File flow, accounting, and database management.

File Flow:

How does your buyer contract travel from pre-tour to post close?

1. _____
2. _____
3. _____
4. _____
5. _____
6. _____
7. _____
8. _____
9. _____
10. _____

What could improve the flow?

_____
_____
_____
_____
_____

New contract file flow systems to employ?

1. _____
2. _____
3. _____
4. _____

How does your listing contract travel from pre-list to post close?

1. _____
2. _____
3. _____
4. _____
5. _____
6. _____
7. _____
8. _____
9. _____
10. _____

What could improve the listing flow?

_____
_____
_____
_____
_____

New listing file flow Systems to employ?

1. _____
2. _____
3. _____

Accounting:

How do you currently account for Income, expenses, and budgeting?

1. Income_____
2. Expenses_____
3. Budgeting_____

What areas of accounting could improve You Inc.?

_____

_____

_____

_____

_____

New Accounting Systems to try/employ?

1. _____

2. _____

3. _____

Database Management:

What systems do you use to handle your contacts, communications, and calendar?

1. Contacts _____

2. Communications_____

   Phone and Answering:_____

   Email System:_____

   Text:_____

3. Calendar _____

What could improve the way you handle:

Contacts?

_____

_____

_____

_____

Communication?

_____

_____

_____

Calendar?

_____

_____

_____

New Database Programs to try/employ?

1. _____
2. _____
3. _____
4. _____

Brand Standards:

List high standards to aspire to in each of the 7 Strategies:

1. Style _____
2. Internet _____
3. Networking_____
4. Brochure_____
5. Advertising _____
6. Direct Mail_____
7. Public Relations_____

Brand Balance:

Name four things to keep each of life's big 3 needs in balance, and then do them.

Body/Health

1. _____
2. _____
3. _____
4. _____

Mind/Mental

1. _____
2. _____
3. _____
4. _____

Heart/Emotional and Spiritual

1. _____
2. _____
3. _____
4. _____

Doodle Box

Brand Adjustments

Consistency

- ☐ Is your style and design consistent in all marketing and advertising pieces that you create and deploy?
- ☐ Does your brand style and design convey a consistent authentic targeted brand message throughout each of the 7 Strategies?
- ☐ Do you have quality brand standard defaults implemented throughout each of your business and strategy maintenance systems?
- ☐ Does everyone that works under your brand adhere to your brand standards and work to advance a consistent brand message?
- ☐ Are the comments that you generate consistent with your intended brand identity and message?

Quality

- ☐ Does your style, design, and standards reflect the quality and message that your brand promises?
- ☐ Have you taken inventory of your brand strategies and your business and strategy maintenance systems?
- ☐ Are you doing everything possible to ensure quality at each client touch point?
- ☐ Does the quality and polish of all your branded digital and print materials reflect your brand passion and promise?

Authenticity

- ☐ Is your brand relevant and compelling to your target niche market?
- ☐ Is there strong alignment between you, your brand, and your target market?
- ☐ Is your life in harmony with the perception of your brand?
- ☐ Are you passionate about both your career and your target market?

☐ Are you living the life that you were meant to live?

☐ Are you keeping the big three in balance: body, mind, and heart?

Accessibility

☐ Are you mentally and physically engaged with your branded real estate business?

☐ Are you easily reachable by your target market, your network, and the media?

☐ Are you committed to living, working, and playing within and around your target market?

☐ Are you the same personable and approachable agent that you originally branded?

☐ Are you actively monitoring brand maintenance systems to see where you can increase branded efficiencies and quality service?

Reinvesting

☐ Are you reinvesting the time for systems review and improvement?

☐ Are you reinvesting at least 15% of your income back into your brand strategies to create further brand acceptance?

☐ Do you continually monitor strategy exposure to better penetrate your target market?

☐ Are you reinvesting time and energy back into your targeted networks?

☐ Are you investing time to stay in balance?

Doodle Box

Branded Agent Help

Visit markhughesbrands.com for more information and tools for discovering, aligning, building, maintaining, and being your powerful personal real estate brand. Our site features industry best branding resources and personal solutions including:

- ✓ Total Branded Agent Solutions
- ✓ Individual Branded Agent Coaching Engagements
- ✓ Branded Agent Workshop Schedules and Registrations
- ✓ Branded Agent Web Site Portfolios
- ✓ Branded Agent Brochure Portfolios
- ✓ Branded Agent Ad and Direct Mail Templates
- ✓ Branded Agent Press Kits
- ✓ Free Branded Agent Newsletter Sign Up
- ✓ Branding Assessment Tests
- ✓ Branded Agent Blog
- ✓ Join the Branded Agent Social Network

Email Mark anytime: mark@markhughesbrands.com